Tomorrow We Fight Yesterday's Men

Lizzie Rose

William Cornelius Harris Publishing

In collaboration

With

London Poetry Books

ISBN 978-1-911232-46-9

William Young

34 Birchwood Close, Bordesley Road SM4 5NH

London Poetry Books

This book is dedicated to all my children and grandchildren.
You are the reason I live and breathe.
You are the reason I know what love is. Always.

With special thanks to Dan and the Hans',
I couldn't have got this far without you, your support means everything to me.

Cover artwork by jest_the_artist_

Contents

Tomorrow We Fight Yesterday's Men

This book is a collection of memories mostly of my own life. Being born in London with two addict parents, growing up in a highly dysfunctional single parent family, being extremely poor and labelled underclass.

Not having the skills to negotiate adult life, I quickly fell into more dysfunctional relationships, leading to domestic violence, mental illness and my own addiction issues.

One constant through all of this has been words. Writing has always helped to manage the chaos in my head. The page has always been a place to leave my memories and to try and make sense of the situations and experiences which have brought me to where I am today.

Although there are a lot of bad moments in my life contained within this book (and not all of them were survived without scars) there is love and lightness here too, life hasn't been entirely bad and it wouldn't be fair to just depress you all now would it? I believe life must have balance.

I have also ventured into writing about people and situations in life like our treatment of nurses, our treatment of refugees and to an extent our treatment of ourselves throughout changing times, is all of our progress in the last fifty years progress?

If I am lucky enough to have you holding this book in your hands, then I truly hope you find something within these pages to connect to, there may be things that we need to survive but it is connection that makes us truly come alive. Connection is the best of the human experience.

When you reach the end, pass me to a friend, give me to a charity shop, leave me on a train or a park bench. I'll survive, I promise.

Ode to a Friend

When the quiet hum
Of an otherwise mundane life
Becomes a scream
That rings in my ears
And I feel I can take no more,

I think on you my friend
And peace restores my life.

Shine

A friend once said something
That struck me in the head
But left me feeling quite
The opposite of dead.

It was something just so obvious
But 'til said out loud doesn't dawn on us.

We walk around with shadows carried
They drain our souls and leave us pallid
Because we accept them as part of how
We navigate the world somehow.

With broken tools and shattered windows
We're usually carrying others sins though.

Instead of believing it will always be
This lurking shadow, this constancy,
Maybe you should hear this thing
That he said to me.

That I'll say to you
And repeat for me.

Maybe it will make a difference
And maybe over time
You'll realise for yourself this line
Darkness can't exist where the sun shines.

Me and Bjork at the Silent Disco

I was wandering through my life
With all its troubles and its strife,
Not really bothering anyone much
Staying vaguely out of touch.
When I picked up a terrible curse
I tripped and fell head first
In lust with a poet,
I didn't really know it at the time
I just thought that he was fine.
But the more I stayed and listened
My eyes began to glisten
And my chest began to swell
He wasn't looking, just as well.

Now I thought that I could cope with
The state of play that now my life is,
The skipped beat that now my heart gives
Every time I see this bliss.
But now my thoughts are keeping me awake
And my dreams, well that's another state
I've tried to push this from my mind
Because poets, well they're a different kind.

The ones that think and see and feel
Provide us comfort, help us heal
They rarely notice souls like me
Sitting in the background quietly.
Actively trying not to be seen
Averting my eyes with a silent scream.
But now he speaks and I'm transfixed
Feeling my emotions mixed
Partly joy, partly dread
Can he see the thoughts inside my head?
Of course he can't, he's carried away
With poetic verse and the themes of the day
He makes it look so effortless.

I am a fan I must confess
That nothing brings me greater pleasure,
Than to hear his words spoken at leisure
To a captive crowd, am I allowed
To say he makes me feel a way?
But sitting in the background here
I start to feel a lack of fear
They're short on poets?!

Well wouldn't you know it
I feel my legs starting to move
I'm feeling in a rhyming groove,
My name goes down upon the list
My stomach balled up like a fist.
But this time I will do it right
Throw poetic verse into the night
Wait now, could this really be?
I think he's staring right at me
I feel exposed and slightly raw
My feet start heading for the door.
But just as I am nearly free
He's standing there in front of me.

He says he likes the stuff I said
These scribblings inside my head,
You should come back he throws on top
And I think I heard my head go pop
Yeah sure, I'm trying to be cool.
But feeling like a teenage fool
Finally I find the door
Good job 'cause I can't feel the floor,

I'm floating home upon a cloud
I finally said my words out loud
In front of him, in front of them
And he told me come back again.
Now lady get your head on straight
He just said hi, it's not a date.
But now he knows who you really are
This beautiful man, this shining star
He shone a little light on me,
On me?! Just 'cause he can't see
What's going on inside my head
It does involve a king-size bed
But wait, don't get ahead of yourself.

I know it's dusty on this shelf
But remember what you said to your heart
From now on I won't take part
In anything not pure and good.
Treat myself just like I should
So I go back 2 times 3 times 4
No longer looking for the door
I make some friends, including him.

And although my head is still full of sin,
I'm finding distraction
In all the reaction
Of people who tell me
That when I speak plainly,
They find a connection
A sort of reflection
Of things they can't share.
But I say you should dare
I came here so long, felt I didn't belong.
But then I stood up, threw my coins in the cup
And it felt really good so you definitely should
Then I thought to myself,

Well wouldn't you know it
I've gone and become a bloody poet,
So much that I didn't see
That he was the one now looking at me.

Saved

Thank you for saving me
In a million little ways you saved me,
In ways that you don't understand
Or realise you saved me.

You saved me when I needed saving,
You saved me when I didn't think
I needed saving, but I needed saving
Or at least redirecting.

Set on the right path or shown the light
And I hope I never need to save you.
But if I do then I'll be there
With my big bag of saves.

Every one you gave to me
Without a thought so graciously,
I saved them all
Just in case you came to call.

Legs

Your leg was touching my leg.

YOUR LEG was touching MY LEG!

Totally accidental
Nothing was intentional.

BUT YOUR LEG WAS TOUCHING MY LEG!

Now there is a temperature
Growing on my thigh, right there.

A heat exchange with lack of air
And now I really am aware.

YOUR LEG IS TOUCHING MY LEG!

Your leg is still as you're engaged
In what we came to see.

Try as I might, I cannot focus
On anything but that heat.

And now there's a cramp
In my left butt cheek.

But I cannot reposition on this seat
Even though my hip,

Is screaming at my knee
YOUR LEG is touching MY LEG you see.

Now at the end of the day
We each go our own way,

With the usual goodbye and take care
Totally, blissfully, thankfully unaware.

But this is where it gets annoying,
Because now it's four in the morning

And I can't sleep
As I'm laying here in this bed
Because in my head,

I can still feel your leg
Touching my leg.

Could I?

I could love you with the heat of a thousand suns
Let a tsunami build in my chest,
With all the cold that's touched my life
You are a fire that burns so bright.

But I am tired and I am empty
I'm broken and afraid,
I keep a bag packed in my head
Filled with all your memories.

Brain tells me you're too good for me
Heart tells me that you'll run,
And then I'll be left with a thousand suns
What do I do with all that fire?

Carry it with me to light my pyre
Or do I set it down?
Stride into the night
Into the darkness to search for more light.

I fear I would never find anyone who
Could light the way as well as you,
But I won't ask you to stay
Truth be told I'm not built that way,

Your happiness is important to me
Even if it is not me,
I will walk away smiling
No sad songs or violins.

For this time that we've had
Will always make me feel glad,
I'll open that bag up once in a while
Look at the memories that made me smile.

And when I finally get
To the end of my road,
You'll find me sitting
On the crescent moon I suppose.

Because as views go
It might be one of the best ones,
To watch the slow setting
Of a thousand suns.

While You're Asleep

Watching you sleep, so still,
Soft between the sheets
All skin and shine, so beautiful.
Limbs curling their way slowly
From one end to the other,
Where your beauty rests
Like the river meets the sea.
Hiding eyes with crashing waves inside,
Beside a dream so plain to see
Your beautiful world laid out before me.
Every inch of perfect skin
The look of you asleep,
So still, so peaceful
Makes my heart race.
I am humbled by such beauty
That I may dare be in this space
Is beyond all that I could dream
I cannot sleep,
So I will sit, so still,
Curled up in this chair.
Watching every breath
That moves your skin
While you're asleep.

The Big Small Hours

I love the way you wrap
Your soul around me
In the form of
Arms and legs,
Then head to neck
You snore into my shoulder.
I love that sound
The comfort of knowing
That you are at rest,
That the shape of me
Fits the shape of you
Well enough, that
Peace is found
In between
Your sleeping breaths.

Kite

Make me a kite
Help me to fly away,
I'm sure it will carry me
I'm really quite light.

No baggage other than
The pain of a million lies,
Treacherous thoughts
Kept behind my eyes.

Just let me soar
Above the sky,
Above this life
For which I do not care.

Just take me there
Above the air,
Where I can see
Untempered light.

Yesterday's Men

Yesterday's men, old soldiers of time
Marching round in my brain
With nowhere to go,
Yesterday's pain lingers with me
As they're crushing me whole
With their boots,
Do we stand up and fight
For this soul we believe?

As time marches on
There's no time left for me,
Just these boots keeping step
In unwanted themes,
And no sleep can I find
No peace in my mind,
Full of soldiers of a war
That's long since lost in time.

But rest while you can
Snatch a portion of dreams,
For another day brings
The same story again,
As tomorrow we fight yesterday's men.

Scared of Myself

I'm scared of myself right now
And I don't know where I'm going,
I don't even know how to get to where I am
And I don't want to be there.

But this is here and here is now
It's not going away, it just grows and breeds
Seeps out around me, surrounds me
Hangs in the air, the scent of my inactivity.

Spawning yet more grief, the loss of a life
Half lived, staring in the mirror
Watching my mother staring back at me
If all the grief that she has seen could speak.

Disgust pours from my eyes
Down my dry face to the well of my hate,
Leaving that shadow behind
On the bathroom wall, painfully.

Down the hall my sadness hurts me
In my bones, in my teeth
And just sitting is not the same anymore

The nothing tires me, the nothing
That leaves no time for anything more,
And sleep won't do its job
I'm never rested, only raw.

Broken

You broke me bodily, quite literally

Left me seeping through the floorboards

I had nothing left to say

You took it all away

Swept under rug all bones and heartbreak

Looking through the cracks

For some shaft of life

Hearing footsteps overhead

Feeling dust settle on my face

Every sound of yours echoes in my head

All the warmth just like a blanket

From above that I can't breach

Too far out of reach

And when you noticed me again

You had nothing left to say

You just threw it all away

Like life was nothing more

Than trash to you.

Can't Sleep

I can't sleep and my heart is heavy
Weighed down with this awake
And all the thought that comes
Between here and now.
Thinking of the vast expanse
Of black outside my window
And wondering how this came to be,
All that's left of me is nearly gone
And I don't know how.

I don't know where to look
To find myself again
I can't sleep and I don't know
Where to go to find such peace.
The power of dream, whispering in my ear
Telling me there's a place, another space
Above the real, just let me steal
An hour of peace to gather up the breaks.

See if it makes a whole unbroken me
The one I left behind in dreams
I can no longer see
I can't sleep and I have no remedy.
Nothing to chase away the night
Or stop the fast-approaching light,
Every watched over sunrise
Breaks my heart.

Reminds me of the part
Behind my eyes
That must endure the
Scorching wake of day
I'm sure someday I will pay,
Because just leaving is not
The same as getting away.

Barricades

Lock the doors
Lock the windows
Check the doors
Check the windows
Check the doors again.

Twitch the curtains
Tweak the shutters
Analyse the mutters
Of strangers on the street
Stay quiet on your feet.

Pull the dresser across the doorframe
Push the drawers against the windowpane
Quiet the panic in your gut
Tape the letterbox shut
Then wait
And listen for the gate.

Watching the windows
Watching the doors
Waiting in silence
Pacing the floors
Praying for daylight.

Alert for the sound
Of splintering wood
And glass on the ground
Of a face in the shadow
You know too well.

Aware that it's bringing
The bruises and swell
The pushing, the squeezing
The hate filled eyes
With scorn and laughter
As they watch your demise.

Crying is too noisy
So stop it right now
No stomach for food
So just go without
Aware that you're.

Hurting yourself
Just like he does,
But in different ways
A real lack of self-love,
But not enough to want to die.

So check the windows
One more time
And wait for the sunrise
Wait for the surprise
You made it once more
To the day, to the light.

So let's do it
All over again tonight.

Run

You have to get out of here
Quicken the pace,

Get to the next street
Now quicken the pace,

Around this next corner
Now quicken the pace,

Keep fast on your feet
Til you find a safe place,

The devil himself
Well he's coming for you,

If you don't believe in the devil
I've got news for you,

He comes dressed like most men
No horns and no tail,

I know sometimes he's female
But mostly he's male,

He'll catch you in moments
When you're all alone,

Then reach for your life
Right down to the bone,

He'll come for you
When you're alone in your bed,

Then leave you stuck there
In your own sticky red,

But he's out on the street now
Close at your heel,

So quicken the pace
Or your life he will steal,

Look for a porchlight
A shop or a car,

Or he'll turn you from flesh
To a fast-falling star,

So quicken the pace
Run if you must,

Or the devil will turn you
From woman to dust.

Holes

At sixteen I found out
What I always knew was true
That I was just a body
To be poured into,

A vessel for the feelings
That you can't control
I'm just a collection of holes,

For your lust, your rage, your jealousy,
You're putting your own stamp on me
And all the while you cannot see
That I am not your property,

This skin does not belong to you
This body that you shudder through
These bones are mine not yours to break,

This flesh of mine not yours to take
But still you press a little more
Then ask me what I'm crying for
You leave before I can reply,

Not caring for the reason why
To you I'm just an empty room
A place to let your ego bloom,

To exercise your fantasy
Of dominance and tragedy
But this soul of mine you cannot break
And my heart was never yours to take,

So I'll wrap them both in linen fine
Remind myself that they're still mine
I'll take them both and make a path,

To where I can forget the past,
A little place all by myself
With a single bed and a good bookshelf
Concentrate on finding me,

Contemplate on being free
Find the things that feed my soul
Fill in the parts between the holes.

Canine

My imagination looks like
A dog waiting to be fed,
Sat in the corner
Staring at me constantly,
She goes wherever I do
Makes a scene or two,
Climbs up on my lap
Makes herself comfortable
Gives me a problem to chew.
She is the gum that sticks
My soul to the floor,
Keeps me looking for the door
She need regular walks
To desolate places,
So no-one can see
Her desperate faces,
Spilling over the edge
Of her tightly done laces.
She's screaming and shouting
And filling up spaces,
She's watching the room
And counting the paces,

With her breath on my heal
It's easy to feel,
Like control is not mine
But she tells me it's fine.

She knows what I want.

She knows what I need.

She knows who I am.

When it's time to feed.

Gem

Great sadness twist this tragedy
Lay out these scars for all to see,
In size and shape and shallow scream
Eager vent this violent dream.

Too many sins I so perceive
Take stride with arrows flight to me,
Make due the pierce I shall receive
My ordered pain knows no reprieve.

Triffid vines cross bitter leaves
Make clear a path for winters breeze,
The rush of air on watered seed
The snowdrop crisp of clarity.

As vengeful fear upon my sleep
The clearest moments shatter deep,
Like sinking ship on calmer sea
My soul does venture down with me.

Hold the Sky

Hold the sky for me,

Save up the time it takes
For me to get to you,
Leave a place by your side
Carved out with my love.

Restore my heart in tiny pieces
Made of photographs and song,
March the winds across my brow
That speak in whispered tones of you.

Let the rain fill up the spaces
Where the sunlight cannot reach,
Washing clean the dusty corners
Of my memories.

I shall wear these shoes
To tread the land
That you were yet to see,
To carry forward all your
Courage, love and dignity.

So hold the sky for me,

Save up the time it takes
For me to get to you,
As I keep a place by my side
Carved out with your love.

(Dedicated to Geraldine Crowe)

1974

I was born on the fashion border
Between hippies and punks
Between old soul and new funk
Between war-time parents
And drop out kids
Between casual racism
And cheap politics.

After women's rights
But not after all of them
You could still assault your wife
But only in the bedroom
And strangers can beat your kids
But only in the classroom.

While we switched over from
Tories gloom to Labour's doom
And some families were still
Living six to a room
When bombings were rife
With political strife.

And miners were striking
And paying the price
From the grey houndstooth coat
To the green bomber jacket
From potatoes in baskets
To mash in a packet.

A lot changed in that era
Leaving make-do-and-mend
For convenience cooking
And the latest new trend,
But all this so-called progress
We think we have had
When I look back on it now
It makes me feel sad.

Some things haven't changed
As much as they should
While others raced forward
Just because they could,
We filled up the world
With single use plastic
If we don't clean it up
The effect will be drastic.

I'm glad I won't be here
To see how it will end
Because I fear it's too late now
To make-do-and-mend,
I know one voice can't change it
And I'm not keeping score
I'm just a girl from 1974.

Superhero

We're judged on how we look
But this is not who we are.

I'm judged for being female
I'm judged for having scars
I'm judged for wearing lipstick,

By every passing dipstick
On a train or in the street
In all the places people meet,

For some I am too quiet
For most I am too loud
For some I am too humble
For most I am too proud.

It's not easy being female
Because you take me as you see me
But if you take the time to find me
You might just see inside me.

You say my jeans are on too tight
You say my heels are far too high.

I say they help me to take flight
And get me closer to the sky
It's a special kind of outfit, a uniform if you like.

Not one for you to fawn over
Or one for you to fight
So throw your shade on me.

I'm busy reaching for the light
In my superhero costume
And today well I just might
Take you down a peg or nine,

With my wonder woman skills
Or I might just walk on by
While I'm feeling super chilled,
Because the hero that's inside me.

Don't care what you have to say
I've heard your petty insults told in every single way.

You're not original in this word game
So get back in your box
Or we could play a little game,

You be the rat, I'll be the fox,
I'll wrap you up in words 'til
You don't know which way is up.

I'll strangle you with language
Then I'll take that trophy cup,
So go on judge me now, I dare you
Tell me just what do you see?

Do I seem like far too much now
Not what you wanted me to be?
A little lady in the background
One that you can judge or you can score,

One you can use for selfish purpose
And then casually ignore.

Well I don't sit so quiet lately
Because I have learned how to fly
So don't interrupt my take-off

Just kiss my arse as I go by.

Sandcastles

Packed like cattle in a rattle tin truck
And pot luck it's you that gets to live,
Scrambling across the fault lines
When you never were to blame,
Heart pain stitched across
Every scar on your frame until,
Colder than cold has ever
Known itself to be
When brothers and sisters
Are claimed by the sea
Because you see they're not free.
Not in their homes
And not in this place,
Herded like wild things
Divided by race,
Washed up on the shores
Of indifferent tides,
A child with no time to choose sides
And detention the prize
For your will to survive.
Drowning in the looks of
A billion eyes,
Gathered and aimed
Through the newspaper lines,
But we're escaping the violence
They're bombing our towns,

Searching our streets
Doing rounds, holding rounds,
Clutching to her breast
The only child she has left.
Women shunted to the right
And men to the left,
Taken in the night
At the government's behest,
Sent back to a place
That filled them with fear,
We feel for you truly
But you can't stay here.
And what of that child
Face down in the sand?
And the beautiful life
His mother had planned,
The front pages echoed
A little boy died,
And all of her dreams
Washed out with the tide
So what price is a life?
What would you risk
If all of your freedom
Came down to this?

Wash Up

Every day there is washing up
Left in my sink

Making you think I don't care
But I do

I know that it's there
Like the dust on the stairs

With the shoes on the floor
And the bags by the door

But I'm fighting a war
And although I agree

It is one you can't see
Nonetheless I still find myself

Sat in this mess
I have to confess

That I'm suffering blindness
To the totems of papers

Collected in corners
Affected by time

As they slump and they heave
I'm learning to weave my way

Back to the door
Where you stand and you stare

At my weakness laid bare
Did I mention I'm fighting a war?

Please don't judge all the times
When I couldn't get up

But you see I was stuck
In a strange kind of nothing

But nothing is something
When you're trying to shift it

I confess I can't lift it or push it away
So I guess it must stay with the dust

And the shoes and the bags and the stuff
I wish I could bluff my way out of this space

But you've seen my place
And you don't look impressed

Also, I'm sorry I'm not dressed
I mean you said you'd be there

But I wasn't expecting
And I don't understand why you care

You should run away quick
Before you fall in the slick

Because I know I will just get the blame
To be honest I am dealing

Well, I'm trying at healing
And I haven't got space for your pain

So while I'm doing the dishes
I have secret wishes that you'll

Just walk right out of the door
Leave me to stress because it is my own mess

I think I mentioned, I'm fighting a war.

Not So Perfect

You are a fantastic mix
Of fabulous and perfect
Like my favourite cocktail,

The one that makes me
Walk funny and smile lots,
The perfect taste that makes

You feel warm and silly
And lots of other pointless things
That feel really good at the time.

But I'm an alcoholic

And I really shouldn't drink you
Because I don't know when to stop,
Then you'll say there's that

Funny walk again
And leave me sitting in the rain
Washed up on the steps

And trying to breathe it off,
Maybe I should leave
Go home and have a cup of tea,

Wait for a dry tide
Or an island somewhere
I hope when I get there,

You won't be waiting for me.

Medical Negligence

We clapped for all the nurses
As they helped the dying die,
We rattled pots and pans
As they watched the living cry.

We promised we'd take care of them
Like they took care of us,
But when it came time for the recompense
We threw them all under the bus.

Sure we made some fancy promises
Like more money in their hand,
But the promises that were made
Didn't quite turn out as planned.

It's like throw the dog a bonus
Keep it happy for a while,
Just as long as you keep working
Stay underfoot, the rank and file.

But when they marched out with their banners
It seems we lost our manners,
You see our gratitude was just a platitude
When they wanted fairness we got really rude.

Get back to your station, just stay in your lane
Clean up all our misery, soak up all our pain
Don't forget to stop at the foodbank
On your weary way back home
From pulling double shifts and crying all alone.

I'm sorry we took so much from you
The ones that kept us living,
We took and took regardless
While you just kept on giving.

But there are limits to a human
And we forgot that's who you are,
That you're healing isn't limitless
We can only push so far.

I for one support your self-care
Because that has to happen first,
Before you can give to others
Your giving must be reimbursed.

I have a Merck Manual on my bookcase
It was called the nurses bible,
And not so long ago
This book was considered vital.

I keep it on my bookcase
To remind me what you do,
To remember all the times
When I needed what you knew.

So I stand in full support
Of the things you're asking for,
It really isn't too much
It didn't need to be a war.

You really shouldn't fight with nurses
One day you'll find yourself in need,
And while they're outside waving banners
Who'll be there to stop the bleed?

Reconcile

Why do we fight in this
Intense non-speaking way?

Why step around the issue
Pretend there's something else to do?

Can you not speak to me
Without getting your head in the way?

Full of if's and and's and but's
And a fear of coming unstuck.
Why not just let your piece be said
And air and clear it out the way?

God knows I've tried to say my piece to you
But you cannot hear me when I speak
And I don't know why it should be hard
You know me inside out.
And all the things we've talked about
But when it comes to you and I
I find a wall between us still.

Why don't we stop this fight
And just be honest without spite
And all the things that come with
Not being true?

Don't you know that deeply still
I always have and always will,
Love you more than all these words
We never seem to say.

Distilled

They distilled me down to a sentence
They told me what I was

They gave my face a name
But I still felt the same

They told me there was help
But they weren't quite sure which one

They said there was no cure
Of that they seemed quite sure

Be careful now, I said
To the people known as they

If I take on all you've said
Then what makes me could be dead

You really should be careful
Not to make this all I am

I am not so much a fan of
All-encapsulating labels

And these fables that you spin
Of other people's lives

That are not relevant to mine
You do not really know me

But you say to me, apparently,
Into the bottle I must go

The one with the funny lid
And the space for my name

You won't feel the same but that's good
You're telling me I should

But you can't tell me who I am
Or where your master plan

Could lead me to
Again I try to speak to you, but apparently

You know more than me
So I guess I'd better go

But just in case you need to know
I have my name and number with me

To explain to the authorities
If the occasion should arise

I'll tell them you know
What is wrong with me.

Afterlife

Fear not my sweet
For when I reach
The gates of no return
I am in the place
Where I shall wait for you
And my finest horse I will send
For when your time comes
And he will bring you safely
To the place where
I shall wait for you.

Other Excellent titles from
London Poetry Books